Living with Intention

To Audrey

you are amazing

Dr. Sonia Noel

Sonia Noel

ISBN-10:1981374345
ISBN-13:9781981374342

Editor and creative director Richard Young
Cover & layout design: Shiv Dindyal
Cover picture: Sean Duncan
MUA: Meleesa Payne
Hairstylist: Corin Gibson

Lashes by: Toya Zepher

Foreword

With esteemed pleasure, I would like to introduce to you a life changing weapon in the form of a book written by Dr. Sonia Noel entitled "Living with Intention".

I've had the privilege of knowing Dr. Noel for several years in the capacity of her spiritual mentor and friend. From this vantage point, I was able to observe her lifestyle and character, and without doubt, her persona is infectious and impacts your life for the better. Dr. Noel is a brilliant, talented, multifaceted individual with a calling to reform her generation. Her profession as a fashion designer and life coach has been an inspiration to many individuals all over the world. She is very optimistic and believes that with God, all things are possible.

In a world where many authors are writing about things that they personally don't know anything about, Dr. Noel stands out as a unique exception since this book is a testimonial of her life's journey. Readers are given an incredible opportunity to travel and identify with her as she reveals her personal struggles, adversities, challenges and also her success stories.

Living with Intention is a book about survival and how to navigate through life's difficult situations. I am confident that after reading, you will be radically transformed and compelled to see life with renewed vision hence, attempting to do things you would have previously thought impossible. It is a device that challenges you to be all that the creator has destined you to be and gives you the thrust that you need to step out from a state of inertia and motivate you to want to live a purpose driven life.

It is my conviction, that if you embrace and practice the principles shared in this book, the world would truly become a better place to live.

Apostle Claude Brooks

Pastor and CEO of Love and Faith World Outreach Ministry.

Dedication

I dedicate this book to the men, women, boys and girls who are still struggling to find and love themselves and strengthen their faith. You can press the reset button now for that positive change.

You will unearth that greatness you possess the day you intentionally decide to grow. Don't rob the world of your amazing contribution.

Acknowledgment

Thank you to God for blessing me with a talent. My family, especially my mom Claudia and daughters Mariska and Shonta for their unwavering support. My adopted son Keron Noble. My spiritual dad, Claude Brooks for your contribution to this book and my journey. My best friend Richard Young for going beyond the call to make this possible. To my loyal and talented graphic designer, Shiv Dindyal, for his exceptional creative skills. To Sean Duncan, you captured that special moment extremely well. To Kidd Marketing for your excellent guidance. My mentors John Maxwell, Lisa Nichols and Les Brown for assisting in giving the world the best version of me. To all the people who sent testimonials, called or sent messages of encouragement or contributed in any way to make this product a reality.

"A few years ago I was asked to introduce Sonia at a speaking engagement and I described her then as an "iconoclast". Today, that word could not be more applicable when one considers her many innovative accomplishments and contributions to her craft and to her country. Guyana salutes you as a true iconoclast Sonia!"

Clinton Urling –
Businessman, Guyana.

Chapter 1

Grow

Determination, faith, focus, self-discipline and consistency can really make anything a reality. Motivation gets us going but discipline keeps us growing, and that is what the law of consistency states and as such has become one of my favourite principles of growth.

Growth is a result of bad habits dropped, wrong priorities changed and new ways of thinking embraced. You cannot grow yourself, if you don't know yourself and you need to learn to lead you, before you can lead anyone else. WOW!

When I am working on projects, this philosophy is constantly on my mind, however, it is not easy to abide by this rule, but we, certainly, can try.

Commit, Contribute, Celebrate

The launch of 'the Love Revolution' was happening right before my eyes at the Pegasus Hotel in Guyana. A unique gathering of people from various races, religions, age groups and political backgrounds, in the same space, sipping 6 Degree wine and juices from Banks DIH.

Prominent politicians, CEOs, teachers, religious leaders, business owners, media personalities, housewives, models, designers and many more were all interacting and having a blast.

I decided to view the gathering from the elevated Victoria lounge, where the musicians were adding an amazing ambience with a special selection of music. Lots of familiar faces and few whom I was seeing for the first time. People were taking pictures with others they knew and even those they were meeting for the first time. This was indeed special. What made it even more special was the first anniversary for a movement I founded, Women Association of Sustainable Development (WASD).

Living with Intention

WASD is a social club providing a forum for business and professional women to relax, renew and rejuvenate while providing support & mentorship to youths and each other.

A feeling of satisfaction overcame me as it felt good to be part of a team that organized this event.

My passion for life was reignited.

I was thinking.......I was growing.

*"You are such a great woman of substance. God is using you for a purpose **and** you have made a great impact on persons' lives as a great role model. You being my mentor has changed my attitude to the bright and positive side and has changed me into who I am today."*

> *Melba Lagaude-*
> *Teacher/CEO Intricate*
> *Creations, Guyana*

*"Sonia Noel has inspired me in so many ways **and** she has such a sweet genuine personality. She always reminds me of how much potential I have, that I can achieve anything, and that the sky is the limit. I call her the modern day Esther from the bible."*

> *Carol Nurse -*
> *Businesswoman, Guyana*

4

Chapter 2

Love

There are many things that the world needs, but more than ever what we need is love, SWEET LOVE. I likened love to a colour, which was so aptly depicted by Richard Young, and so the Love Revolution was born.

"The colour of love radiates from a much centered space and an omnipresent time! Grounded in the essence of the universe as all-providing, this natural vibe is transcendent, permeating all bigotry, bias, and barrier. Its ethos is rooted in liberation and liberty and its range of emancipating elements define our textured and triumphant existence. Earth and Nature enliven its soul, in their ever-evolving hues, making us earthy, natural and above all, loving! This is the LOVE REVOLUTION, colouring our world in warm tones of sunrise yellow, sunset orange, terracotta soil and rainforest green."

My spiritual dad and mom pastor Claude and Carol Brooks opened the evening proceedings with prayers.

We had some special performances with a love theme, rendered by talented singers and musicians - Rashleigh Joseph, Ras Camo, Max Masiah, Miriam Corlette-Williams and Natalie Major. The master of Ceremony was my dear friend, Merrano Issacs, who lent his perfect broadcasting voice which added to the classy touch at the occasion. All evening, there were many quotes from various personalities about love and compassion depicted on the screens.

I briefly shared my vision, a personal story and my why for this event, making way for our guest speaker, Dr. Linda Wallace. I closed with a famous quote from an extraordinary human being, an amazing leader and one of my mentors, Mr. Nelson Mandela, "No one is born hating another person just because of the colour of his skin, or his background, or his religion. People have to learn to hate, and if they can learn to hate, they can be taught to love, for love comes more naturally to the human heart than its opposite."

Not hating the world after his incarceration for over twenty-five years and moving from prisoner to president, is an absolutely amazing feat. What an extraordinary human being he was.

Dr. Linda Wallace is a pastor from California, an empowerment specialist, an author, and a women's rights advocate. Her presentation motivated the audience and many people interacted with her throughout the evening.

I met Linda in California at the launch of the Women's Code event hosted by Carla Sorenson Jackson, just a few months before this event. There was an instant connection, after my friend and well known Nigerian jewellery designer Monalisa Okojie introduced us.

When I told my friend Anna and Mona I was coming to California, I knew they thought that I was joking but I told myself 2016 had to be explosive and more than that, I had a plan.

A list of influential women was in attendance, including business coach Anna McCoy, actresses - Angie Harmon, Garcelle Beauvais and 'Married to Medicine' star Lisa Nicole Cloud and many more. I had a special connection with Linda, for she possessed that calmness with a heart full of love.

We would always have inspiring conversations and one day, I was sharing some plans with her and she was listening intently. And then she said I think you will start a love revolution and I will be there to support you.

I am very proactive, so in a matter of days, together with my team, we had a plan. It was a feeling of excitement when she agreed to come and I was thinking God has to be placing people in my life to assist me with my journey. I was ecstatic she was coming but I was curious about what motivated her to buy her ticket to come to some place of which she knew very little.

This was the response to the question. She said she was impressed with me but she went on to proclaim the ultimate source which is our heavenly father for his divine answers.

She sent me a rationale - Who is Sonia Noel and what is in her heart for the daughters in Guyana?

"Sonia Noel is one of my champions for the cause of humanity but specifically for the development of people. She is a voice that represents my Kingdom but is speaking on behalf of my heart for the nations and the region of the Caribbean. I am elevating her in spiritual authority, wisdom and aligning her with a new movement of women (the remnant) that I will strategically use to mobilize a revolution that will be motivated out of love and service and compassion for mankind. The momentum will increase, and visibility will increase for I am positioning her to the highest levels of influence where she will with grace and dignity challenge the policies and traditions of men to advocate for the poor and for those who do not have a voice. She is using every platform to promote and impact the cause of women, children and families. She recognises that through the empowerment and mobilisation of skilful women she can influence the economic climate within her country and beyond her borders. I am favouring her but and also filling her with the passion and stamina to initiate a new standard of life and living. She represents beauty, eloquence and discretion. Much like Esther her beauty - in spirit captures the attention and the heart of decision makers. Through her. My purposes for the daughters of Guyana will advance, creating global platforms and positions for them to occupy new territory and bring the intelligence that I have placed in them to a new level of power and glory. Seemingly what has been in obscurity (women of Guyana) is being displayed now for the glory and fame of my name. These women have been quietly preparing themselves and a nation for a revolution that will shift the economies and markets of this world.

They will emerge with one voice and one intent to establish the values and principles of integrity, honour and demand to participate in an economy that secures the future of their nation and future generations. It will surprise many as they have been known as a people with a gracious, quiet demeanour but I am causing an awakening and stirring among them which will be led by my daughters, who will contend in prayer, develop strategies, implement policies and mobilize a call to action."

"Hi Sonia. I have to tell you how much I admire the work you've been doing. I know you're an amazing designer and I proudly wear your pieces but I'm now even prouder to wear them knowing how much you're transforming lives. So proud to know you and love you."

- Dr. Tanya Destang, St Lucia.

"Miss Noel is a straightforward tell-it-as-it-is person. She is selfless and doesn't stop when she encounters problems. She possesses and portrays qualities of a great role model."

Chris Piper -Welder, Trinidad

Chapter 3

Mission

With tears in my eyes and completely speechless, my reaction was WOW! It was an absolute honour, and I was flattered. I asked myself if I were deserving of this big responsibility and if I were able to deliver. "Is this part of my mission?" So many questions started flooding my mind.

Nevertheless, the feedback was very positive and many persons felt that these types of events were needed to forge meaningful relationships in the society. We created a button for branding on which the love revolution logo was inscribed and everyone in attendance received one. The idea was for them to pin it on someone while saying why love is important to the world and encourage the receiving person to do the same.

I started questioning myself as to the way forward and the best way to utilize my talent to serve. My creative mind is difficult to shut off because God has given me a talent. I was fortunate to be blessed with being given the opportunity to serve. How do I know it is a gift? I love what I do and I am good at it. Now, I also have an opportunity to use it.

It is my mission.

Using my gift to enhance lives is so gratifying and I also knew I had to be healthy in my mind, body and soul to serve effectively. Hence I hired Roger Callender, a personal trainer, to assist with my physical fitness before embarking on my next Women in Business Expo project.

The idea was for Sonia Noel Foundation to collaborate with WASD. All businesses have challenges but small businesses like mine can crumble if we don't get creative at keeping it afloat.

The Sonia Noel Foundation for Creative Arts (SNFCA) was formed just over five years ago and its vision is to create access for talented individuals, not only in Guyana, its home base, but throughout the wider Caribbean. Since then, the Foundation has partnered with varying social and charitable entities and has raised funds for causes such as Sickle Cell, Breast Cancer, Children with Disabilities and Autism.

I received a call from my best friend, Richard Young who has the best creative mind I have encountered thus far, expressing that his business partner and former Miss Trinidad and Tobago, Nicole Dyer Griffith, wanted to host a motivational event for women. She was also a former Minister in the Trinidad government and a prominent women's activist.

The event was slated to commemorate International Women's Day and would celebrate the achievements of women while also looking to accelerate gender equality. We immediately started planning for an empowering weekend to celebrate all women. With no funds allocated for the events, my team was wondering where these funds were coming from. I assured them confidently that this weekend of activities will not only be a reality but will change lives.

We decided not to have a cost for exhibitors participating in the expo because we did not want money to be a deterrent for them not having the opportunity to expose their businesses. The expo was also free to the public. All the projects hosted by SNFCA over the years were financed from my personal resources and kind-hearted friends, who contributed because they saw what a difference it was making.

I had to be extra creative and innovative to make this happen in a short time. I had recently enrolled in the John Maxwell University which needed a lot of my time and then there were my usual travels. How was I going to do this? I kept repeating I can do, I can do, I can do, we can do it, we can do it, and we can do it!

Chapter 4

Bold

The word bold is synonymous with my name and I can be convincing when I move into action mode especially when it involves doing things for others. The words of John Maxwell are constantly in my ears. "Success is when I add value to myself. Significance is when I add value to others". My small but effective and loyal team include: Caribbean fashion guru, Richard Young, Keron Noble, (my adopted son), Shiv Dindyal, Eric Phillips, Meleesa Payne and my two daughters Marisca Fiedtko-Jordan and Shonta Noel. I am aware sometimes I drive them crazy because I know their abilities and I want to see them achieve maximum potential. I don't accept words like - impossible, can't, shouldn't, mustn't, no etc. I love and appreciate them so much and I know the feeling is mutual.

Both events were extremely successful and we had a lot of media attention because it was amongst the biggest events for women's month. The testimonies made some of us emotional that we made such a huge impact on lives in a personal and professional way. During the planning I mentioned to my team we should visit the women in prison because they need some motivation to continue to dream. I had visited them a year prior and promised I would return. We decided to create a book marker with a special message relevant to International Women's Day as a special gesture and as usual, my friend Richard coined these empowering words.

Women are Dynamic

Women are Creative

Women are Versatile

Women can make a difference

Women are Unique

Women are Innovative

Women are Resilient

Women can change the world

Living with Intention

Women are Enterprising

Women are Risk-Taking

Women are Evolving

Women can chart their own Destinies

Women are Believers

Women are Healers

Women are Lovers

Women can save our community

Women are Motivators

Women can save our Humanity

Women are Mentors

Women are Mothers

Women can rise to the Occasion

Commit, Contribute, Celebrate

I was accompanied there, by talented actress Sonia Yarde and Florence Bourne, both members of WASD.

An expo T-shirt and a booklet was in each gift package. We felt so gratified for our offering was so highly appreciated by the inmates.

I encouraged them that the reset button to their lives is always an available option. I stressed the need to be Bold.

Chapter 5

Mindset

"It is vital to your wellbeing to keep a positive mindset and don't give up on your dreams because of this temporary situation. Do not conform to the pattern of this world, but be transformed by the renewing of your mind. Then you will be able to test and approve what is God's will — his good, pleasing and perfect will." Romans 12:2

"You are in here now and I know many of you have brilliant business ideas and we will welcome you in the future to join the EXPO. Continue to see yourself not where you are now but what you could be in the future." These were my parting words to them. I asked the two pregnant women, present, to send me a message about the birth of their babies so I could visit the hospital, as promised.

We all deserve a second chance in life and giving hope to someone can make a difference in their lives.

As I was leaving, and the iron gates closed behind us I remembered a quote I saw online which said "If you want to touch the past, touch a rock. If you want to touch the present, touch a flower. If you want to touch the future, touch a life". — Unknown

On our way back to the city from Berbice, I was thinking about the fact that some of the young ladies in the prison were the same age or even younger than my daughters, Marisca and Shonta. This thought led me to reflect on my dearest daughters. I am so proud of these two girls and I thank God for them every day. I have two biological daughters but have a few others who call me mommy like Rudiana, Sarifina, Anasha and Zoe. I often wonder how I did it and many people have asked me the same question, considering life's circumstances. I consistently struggled to find that balance of motherhood and career. Is that balance even possible? As a single parent with two daughters, I've experienced many challenging days but because of my Faith in God and a positive mindset I endeavoured to persevere.

Over the years I tried to be the best mother I could be while building my brand, adding value to myself and others. My daughters constantly express what a wonderful mom I am, in spite of the fact that I missed some of the most important moments in their lives because of travelling, often for work. There were times I did not feel that wonderful but I comforted myself knowing I was giving my best shot. I did what I did then, with what I knew then, to be the best mom.

When I think about it, I had no choice but to be the best mom I could be because of the example I had. Claudia Noel-John, my mother, epitomizes 'a phenomenal woman'. She survived under extreme difficult situations but kept her five kids together, after leaving a very abusive marriage.

I was her first born, followed by my sister Nicole, brothers Shawn, Sherwin and Shermon. She later gave birth to my baby sister Denielle, when she remarried to a very loving man, Allan John, who was a father to us. She was determined even when my dad decided not to support us financially nor otherwise. My mom said she would never let us down. She was left without anything just so her children would have. Even though we had little, she made us feel like we were full of value.

Also my grandmother, Winifred, my aunts and other members of the extended family were always very supportive. When you have that kind of support structure, it prevents women from returning to abusive relationships.

My babies have grown into such beautiful, intelligent, loving and well-rounded young women of whom I am totally proud. They possess different personality types, for sure, yet they both developed such a close relationship. People often ask me what is the recipe and my answer is always the same. "You have to give your kids that solid foundation of believing in love and by extension believing in God." I impressed upon them that they must believe they have the ability to achieve anything and that they should give the world the best version of themselves while respecting others. Also share and live based on the law of intentionality which defines that growth is the only guarantee that tomorrow will get better. You cannot rise above your mental condition if you don't change your mindset and see beyond what you are, presently.

*"There **are** so many things about Sonia Noel ...but the passion for life, the passion that she has for helping people motivates me, and she is always ready to help, always pushing you to be the best version of yourself"*

- Vanda Allicock-Indigenous Designer,Guyana.

"The first time I saw you, your hair caught my attention. I was instantly interested in who that eccentric woman was. During our conversation I saw a glimpse of your passion, your drive and your love for what you do and most of all why you do it. Your inspiration for me is the way you love to see young women succeed. Sonia Noel, admire your strong faith in Jesus and how it's not an obstacle in anything you do but an opportunity to teach others."

❤- Chan Tale Flood – Designer, Suriname

Chapter 6

Pride

I always tell persons, including my girls, the outside can always be fixed but we need to work on the inside and finding yourself. There will always be challenges along the way, but no matter what, find a way to serve humanity, ultimately. When you fail, fail forward. It is all a matter of pride.

They both have independent views and are not afraid to voice them, without fear. Marisca was a passionate student of medicine, at one time, however, through a curious turn of fate, she later became interested in the oil sector. I have never forced anything on my kids because they have to live their lives and they need to make their mistakes. They both are interested in politics and the developments of our country. On occasion, they both attend parliament sessions, and on another occasion, I have witnessed them, especially

Marisca, in heated political debates with friends and holding their own. I looked at her one night when she was in her element and remembered I almost lost her.

Over 23 years ago, I was walking out of the children's ward with tears running down my face as my daughter Maric a was crying and screaming "MOMMY, MOMMY, MOMMY!" I walked down those stairs and into the yard where I could still hear her crying, more so because her crib was at the window and she was watching me. I looked back at the innocent, tiny, pretty thin face that was looking at her mommy leaving her with people she had never seen, before. It was always me and her everywhere. For a few years well, I seldom went places that I could not take my baby.

Many kids were in the hospital, that time, with Gastroenteritis, so, unfortunately, two children were placed in one small crib. I felt so helpless sitting there for hours waiting for someone to look at her. As Gastro was threatening my daughter's life, all I could do was pray that God would spare her life.

I had promised my baby and myself, while she was still in my belly to be a great mom. At that moment, I did not even feel like a good mom much less a great one. I was living in Bartica, then, but because she was so ill, she needed to get to the city as soon as possible.

I ended up staying at one of my relatives in Georgetown, who was not too thrilled to have a family member there with a sick baby and moreover, little funds. But I had few options, afforded me, at that time, and her dad was not a part of her life financially nor otherwise. The following morning, I returned to find my daughter and the other baby playing in their excrement. It broke my heart that I could not take her to a private hospital with better facilities. I visited my baby as often as I could because I was not allowed to stay with her.

Two days later, the beautiful little girl sharing the crib with my daughter sadly died. OMG! I was panicking as I looked at her alone in the crib, very weak but happy to see me. Those are moments you wished that the father was there so you don't feel so alone.

Two decades ago, not everyone had a telephone line in Bartica, so I had to call my cousin to give my mom a message about what time I was going to call her. I spoke to her once a day and she was so assuring. My mom knew well of what I was going through because she had been in similar situations, many a time. Fortunately, I learnt from someone about Children Praise Hospital and I decided to check it out and moved her there. She was better within 24 hours and I finally started relaxing a little. Her doctor's name was Dr. Michael Sear and he was so kind to us and in a few days she was discharged. We couldn't wait to get back to Bartica to be with my mom and other siblings where the LOVE was overflowing. Looking back, I realized that incident made me more determined to be in a better position to take care of myself and my baby.

My amazing daughter, Marisca now has a precious son, Jaidyn Jordan whom I adore. She is a remarkable mom who I admire very much. I know there are lots of mothers, especially single mothers, out there that can relate to this story or something similar. Sometimes we have no idea how strong we are until being strong is the only choice you have. I thought about the little girl and many others who did not make it and feel so blessed that God protected her. She is a great mom and mentor to her brilliant almost six-year old son who adds so much joy to my life.

My younger daughter, Shonta contributed to one of proudest moments in my life when she was awarded best business student in the Caribbean, for Caribbean Advanced Proficiency Examination (CAPE). We travelled to Belize for the award ceremony and that evening when professor Hillary Beckles said, "can the parents of the brightest minds in the region please stand?" I stood with tears in my eyes as I looked at my baby on stage with the other academic stars of the Caribbean.

She has always been so disciplined and intentional in everything she does. She had told me a year before that she was going to be head girl, valedictorian and best student and she did it. She worked hard to get there. She gave up social media and other interests to concentrate on her exams.

She even refused to accompany me to a resort, for a holiday, because of her self-discipline. Even now, I look at her and I know I was not that focused when I was her age. She puts a very high value on time and what she does with her 24 hours. As they say, time is the greatest equalizer.

I feel blessed that both of my daughters have a heart for giving and they both possess WILL power and WHY power.

Will and Why power was the driving force behind climbing to the top of Stone Mountain with my friend Doreen. We all have that 24 hours, no matter where we come from, but the difference is how we utilize those hours.

Having a sense of pride in what you do keeps you energized to keep doing.

Chapter 7

Inspire

This really is fantasy land, I thought as I look at the outline of Disney World from my balcony at the Marriott World Center in Orlando. I promised my grandson, Jaidyn we will have lots of fun there one day.

To think Walt Disney was fired from the Kansas City Star in 1919 because his editor said, he "lacked imagination and had no good ideas." Imagine if he had allowed that person's opinion to define him? I would not be looking at this spectacle. Stories like this inspire us all.

It was my birthday and I was there for the John Maxwell International Certification program. Last year for my birthday I spent with immediate family, close friends and the seniors in my church. It was one of my most memorable birthdays.

One month before my birthday I woke up with a clear message where I needed to be and with whom.

When I met with Sister Beverley to discuss the plans for my 44th birthday, she was ecstatic and she was more excited about the makeovers planned for all of the seniors. On the 15th of August they arrived at Herdmanston Lodge between 9:00 and 9:30 a.m. for the special pampering in preparation for the brunch.

My Leo brother, Richard Young had just celebrated his birthday and was assisting with the makeovers.

My friend Shiv was the photographer and was capturing everyone as they entered. One of my favourite musician's Camo had a great selection of music that welcomed these men and women who mean so much to me. Most of the seniors were wearing clothing from my collection and a few from other local designers.

I was in awe when I saw my guests coming in to take their seats. Truly a transformation! Some of them, I did not recognize because even the hairstyles were changed. Some ladies expressed they had not applied makeup since their wedding day. The happiness and excitement was evident as they moved to the music. Jennifer did a powerful spoken-word presentation. This scenario is what I envisioned for my special day. When my friend Russell Lancaster and Shawn English sang I got so emotional that I hugged Richie and cried. Apostle Brooks was thrilled to see the happy expressions displayed on the senior's faces.

I received so many hugs and 'I love you' statements, that day, enough to last me a lifetime.

They all left with a gift bag after having a delicious non-alcoholic wine and few ladies received a framed picture.

Since that day when I attend church the overflowing love I receive energizes me for days. They would also notice if I missed a Sunday. The entire occasion was indeed extra special for one of the ladies who passed a few months later. Her daughter sent me a message expressing heartfelt thanks because her mom celebrated her last birthday in style.

Creating precious memories and maintaining lasting relationships are priceless episodes of life's blessings. So it is our obligation to constantly inspire.

As I admired the illuminated park I thought about having fun with my grandson in the near future. Although I was alone I did not feel alone because I just had hundreds of people whom I never met before singing "happy birthday" to me. The pianist also did a special rendition of happy birthday. It's a great feeling to feel loved and appreciated and also to reciprocate.

I felt welcomed into the John Maxwell Team and I was bursting with exciting possibilities for my future. Over one hundred flags lined the corridor and I could not help but to take a photo next to my country's flag, the Golden Arrowhead. I was proud that it was there because of my participation.

Next morning, I went down early for breakfast with great anticipation for a fabulous first day of the conference. Persons were so friendly and engaging and the JMT executives had the most wonderful welcome planned and so well executed. We had our table number and were assigned a pleasant mixture of persons from various backgrounds. Jan Roberts from South Africa and I were the two at our table that were not from the United States of America and we kept in touch after the conference more than anyone else at the table. We shared some details about ourselves, marveling that we had varying backgrounds and professions. Not surprisingly though, I was the only person with a career in fashion at the table and I encountered no other for the duration of the conference.

I was celebrating almost two decades in the Guyanese fashion industry and also as one of the more recognizable names in the directory of Caribbean fashion. At this moment, I was finding a way to redesign my life. Most times when people think of the Caribbean, they think mainly about sand and sea but there is much more to us than that. We have a very rich culture which depicts in our performing arts. The abundance of talent which we possess within that small region is so amazing. Fashion and music are becoming more and more internationally relevant, in recent years.

Talking about music, I remember clearly Barbadian RHIANNA coming to my shop in Barbados, and how proud I was in acknowledging that her mother is from my homeland Guyana. Look where she got to! Now here I am! Imagine, that small town girl from a tiny mining town of Bartica, up the Essequibo River, with big dreams and believing it was possible, now in a room with more than three thousand people from around the world for the International Certification Program. Wow! Everything is possible!

When the Maxwell team committed to adding value to lives, they are not joking. I was blown away by the level of professionalism and content. John Maxwell is super blessed with a dynamic team of executives, speakers and coaches that is second to none and it was an honour to be part of this family. Dr. John Maxwell is an

American author, speaker, and pastor who has written many books, primarily focusing on leadership. Titles include The 21 Irrefutable Laws of Leadership and The 21 Indispensable Qualities of a Leader.

"Sonia is a unique, talented and confident woman and has a warmth about her that makes anyone who comes into her presence feel at ease. No matter what the situation is, her calm spirit is contagious. Truly beautiful inside and out, always ready to make others feel and aspire to bring the best in others by believing in themselves. She is an inspiration to women across borders"

> *-Isabelle Doll-Nycobo-Artistic Director/PR Consultant, South Africa*

Chapter 8

Focus

By the end of the first day I was bursting with new meaningful contentment. I was anxious to share with whomever I encountered. I started sharing information on my social media and people were responding positively, which was encouraging. We all just need a little coaching to nudge us in the direction to enhance our lives. We need always to have focus.

After a delicious dinner I opted for a hot shower, opened my favourite bottle of Moscato from Royal Wines and I smiled while sipping and feeling absolutely grateful.

Sonia, you have certainly come a far way, my lady, I told myself as my mind drifted to what it took to get me on this accelerated intentional journey. Most of my life I had been unconsciously intentional, however conscious that I can raise my sense of self. I remember like it was just a few weeks ago, what triggered the conscious intentionality

The stunning reflection in the mirror that was looking back at me as I prepared for New Year's Eve church service, at Love & Faith Outreach Ministries in 2015, comes to mind. An up-close look at the eyes showed some sadness but one had to look deep to see the determination.

My elaborate purple skirt with lattice around the bottom was cascading like the rapids in my country, Guyana. My signature latticing formed a V see through panel up the left side. The top was fitted with one sleeve and transparent around the upper chest area. My makeup was done professionally and I was sporting a cute short black hairstyle instead of my long blond signature braids. As I viewed myself in the mirror, I realized how tall I was because of the beautiful suede 6 inch heels. The reflection was flawless but the inner me was in turmoil.

The year 2015, I started being more real with Sonia. I realized that although I was purposeful and focused, I needed to accelerate my growth plan because growth just doesn't happen without a plan. The law of intentionality says growth is the only guarantee that tomorrow will get better and do better. We all experience growth gaps to prevent us from achieving our greatness. It can be an assumption that growth is automatic. Sometimes we know we need to grow but knowing how can be a problem. Maybe you don't think you have a growth environment but get started as there is never a perfect time to start. Just get started!

Like Jim Rohn said "You cannot change your destination overnight, but you can change your direction overnight."

I was at a crossroad and had to make certain decisions to the direction of my life and make changes to my relationship with God and man. Changes in my business, relationship, health etc. had to be done. Self-reflection, most of the time, puts things into perspective and the picture was becoming clearer. I had to face reality that my relationship with someone I loved dearly and who I know loves me in the only way he knew how, was coming to an end. It was sensible, at that time, to accept that the season was over, for life is about seasons. Was I devastated? Very much and what made it harder is we knew each other for two decades. We were close friends and I often asked myself if crossing the line was a good idea. A wonderful guy, indeed, and we had memorable times together but circumstances prevented the relationship from going any further. I tried to be as real with myself as possible, because we had those moments. Nevertheless, we chose to be in denial to avoid the pain. During those months, I had to get to know me more and love me more. I am a very positive and strong-willed person but matters of the heart can weaken the strongest of us.

I always challenged myself to keep focused. It does not come easy.

My daughters Marisca and Shonta were preparing for their New Year's Eve house party with friends, as I came down the stairs. They complimented me on how beautiful I looked and they hugged me and expressed their love and appreciation that I was the sole parent that was part of their lives.

He was sitting next to me on our way to church and I was experiencing a strange feeling in my gut that was so uncomfortable. As we entered the church, the worship songs hit me and I began to feel better. My Love & Faith family was greeting and complimenting me. If they only knew that the interior did not match the exterior. It was the worst I felt in recent times, but it was comforting knowing my God is awesome.

Apostle Claude Brooks's sermon was on point and it touched my core. I got emotional a few times before midnight and I was happy the lights were dim so tears streaming down my face was not noticeable.

By midnight I could not control myself and I let it go to new beginnings. I had this conviction that 2016 would be a life changing year, by God's grace. I was determined to spend more time with family and importantly more time with God. We find time to get to know people with whom we are desirous of developing a relationship and the same must go for our relationship with God. I felt there was a greater purpose for my life.

I got home about 12:30 am and the party was in full swing with my daughters and their friends. I said happy New Year to them and headed to my room in a haste to be alone. The tears were flowing like the Orinduik Falls. The last time I cried like that was when my grandmother died. Have you ever done a really ugly cry? With snat running out of your nose?

I let everything out. I don't like loud music but I appreciated it because I did not want my daughters to worry about me. Someone once asked me if I ever cry because I seem to have it all together. None of us has it all together for we all, at some point, go through darkness and rough spots. We may even feel like we hit rock bottom but there is always a silver lining.

I woke up on the first day of the New Year knowing I loved me and life even more.

I forgave myself for many things which cause a heaviness to go.   Knowing better things are in my future. I took a deep breath and took a minute to acknowledge and appreciate my organs for the amazing work in keeping me functioning. One thing on the top of my mind was accelerating my growth plan because by adding more value to me was at the top of my agenda. That is the only way I would be able to add value to others. "The people who do not grow are unwilling to leave what they have known and practised. They are not willing to admit wrong so they can discover what is right, therefore they cling to right, and their lives turn out wrong. Surrendering being right is a prerequisite to being right."

-John Maxwell

Style is distinctive
Style is classic
Style is perennial

Some of us are born with style
Some of us cultivate style
Some of us become style

But....

Style has no purpose if there is no meaning
Style has no value if there is no mandate
Style has no soul if there is no mission

Richard Young – Fashion Evangelist

Susie Carder and Lisa Nichols, Les Brown,
Linda Wallace and Pastor Carol Brooks,
Actress Anna Horsford.

Singer Michelle Williams (former Destiny Child), Iyanla Vanzant, Women in Business Expo and Kathy Kidd.

My daughters Marisca and Shonta, my
grand-son Jaidyn, Claudia John (Mom) and
my adorable puppies.

With Roderick from the special Needs School.

Enjoying a moment with my foster kids

My birthday with the seniors from my LOVE & FAITH

At church New Year's Eve

With 96 years old aunt Lou who is the oldest person in my hometown Bartica.

At the top of Stone Mountain in Atlanta with Doreen.

Commit, Contribute, Celebrate

"You are a woman of value, purpose and integrity. You represent the masculine and feminine line power in balance. You inspire others through love, compassion and kindness!"

- *Bethany Love-*
  Businesswoman, Arizona.

Chapter 9

Faith

I was willing to jump again, to take a leap of faith, believing my parachute will open but if it did not open, I would develop, that mindset to deal with it because I was learning to feed my faith and starve my fear. When you get to know you better, you realize courage is a door that can only be opened on the inside. I have been digesting lots of John Maxwell materials and I realized most of his content was influenced by the Bible, I was becoming even more interested. I was sure, at this point in my life, I needed to be selective as to what I listened to, about what I read and the people around whom I surrounded myself.

I dare you to take a closer look at your inner circle. Who is in your front row? Are they deserving of that position? Do they genuinely care about you?

Can you trust them? What are they contributing to your life?

It is hard to let people go sometimes but it can be the best decision for both parties. Not everyone is going to take that journey with you. The fallouts may even be family members.

I needed to enrol in the John Maxwell online campus. I decided that the people around me and the activities in which I engage must contribute in a positive way to my journey.

The more I thought about it, the more convinced I was that I needed to take action. I knew I was going to do the course no matter what. I knew my WHY but not clear on my HOW. This is what faith is all about.

What is your WHY for doing the things you do?

I began looking at the different payment options trying to determine what is possible, considering that it was January. There was a special offer - if you enrolled between a certain dates and kept the payment plan, your hotel would be complimentary. Sounded like a deal I needed desperately. It was a bit challenging to get the down payment because I had a few financial obligations personally and business wise. I kept reassuring myself it would be fine because my faith is very strong. When a friend promised to assist me with the payments, things seemed to be coming together and I was so excited to peruse the online university.

It was so difficult sometimes to get access to the live calls because of the weak internet connection in Guyana so I accessed the recorded calls. I made up my mind I will persevere.

Real growth happens when we are at our lowest, feeling vulnerable and undergoing huge discomfort. I was adding value to me and it felt amazing. I spent hours reading and listening earnestly to John's Material. Every day I read, listened and wrote the things that were good food to my soul and mind. Intention has to be backed up by good actions for us to see the results. We need to move from good intention to good action.

Apart from John, there were other motivational speakers and transformation coaches, Les Brown and Lisa Nichols who became my living mentors in the self-development business. The late Dr. Myles Munroe and Wayne Dyer impacted my life in such a major way also.

Being able to share some content from the university and from the books with family, friends and members of the Women Association for Sustainable Development was so empowering. All of the personal development books that I owned, I lent to persons. I called it the relay method of passing the books on. I have a list of people waiting on them to be returned. I believe, wholeheartedly, in taking other persons with me as I advance. It is better than doing it alone. To have a collection of great books does not achieve much in my office. I received many testimonies of the shift of focus, many persons experienced after reading those books. My aunt Brenda told me after reading '15 Invaluable Laws of Growth' that she wished someone had introduced that book to her 10 or 15 years ago and her life would have been different.

Chapter 10

Purpose

It was becoming evident that the internet was not the only problem arising as a deterrent to my course but payment. The commitment from my friend who had pledged to sponsor fell through and it was devastating because I wanted this so badly. Have you ever wanted something so bad you can feel the end result, but there were so many things keeping you from the finish line?

This is when you are beginning to know your purpose.

The feeling of depression started creeping in because my finances were tied up so I could not pay it at that moment. If there is one thing you will learn about me is I have a high comeback rate so the depression that was trying to step in, was only successful for a few seconds.

Saying to myself that I am painting on the canvas of life like the geniuses Pablo Picasso and Giotto di Bondone, made me resilient. I made the decision what colour to use and I decided what size of the brush that would create the images of my life. That was powerful.

I am also a lion. Come on lion, go hunt!

The Bible mentions the lion is an amazing creature and has the leadership attitude. The lion is not the largest, tallest, heaviest or smartest of the animal kingdom but the king of the jungle. Have you ever asked why? I love looking at pictures of lions. There is a calmness they possess even when danger is in the vicinity. Myles Munroe said "An army of sheep led by a lion will always defeat an army of lions lead by a sheep." The lion is the king of the jungle because of attitude, respected by all. This analogy shows that no one should have excuses that they can't because of what they don't have. Your belief system can make you fail or succeed. The lion is the king because he thinks and convinces everyone he is the king.

I told myself I was not a Leo by accident and I am in charge of the jungle. The lioness is the one that hunts for her family so I need to go hunting. Adversity was motivating me. There are always positives and benefits in bad experiences and we can find them if we look. Who can do this for me without compromising myself? Who is that someone who would pay the balance of my tuition and I would pay them back. I asked God to guide me on this one. A few names came to mind but I gravitated to someone I respected and who respected me. We were not the same race, sex, age, nor religion.

I called and he was in office and I was there in half an hour. I laid my cards on the table and I looked him in the eyes and said I can't give you a date when I will repay you but I will give you my word that I will and my word is my bond. Without hesitation Mr. Mohamed asked for the bank transfer info and in 24 hours the university sent a confirmation email that the balance was paid. He could have said no but he did not. He commended me for not having a quitting attitude and my desire to continue serving others. Credibility and integrity are vital and I don't ever intend to lose those values.

I spent extra time with God that night asking Him what he was preparing me for. What is my assignment? I knew it had to be beyond my imagination. I prayed not only for myself but for those persons experiencing difficulties and those feeling helpless, living in search of their true purpose.

To let my passion to succeed and overpower my fear to fail, became my mantra. For even if we fail at something, it does not make us failures. And it is not a matter of if we will fail but when we will fail. Overcoming failure, that's the crux of the matter! Fear can paralyze us but we need to turn it around and make it our fuel. I love this definition someone shared about FEAR (False Evidence Appearing Real). Adversity motivates me. There are always positives and benefits in encountering bad experiences and we can find them if we look hard enough.

I spent some time alone reflecting. I had another situation. When I registered there was a deal of accommodation covered for the live event providing you paid within a certain time frame, which I defaulted on. The cost was close to USD$ 1000 which I did not have to spare. The only way to find out is to be bold and honest and that I was. I called the office in Florida and they said they were not sure of what is possible but would get back to me.

When I completed that call, I felt to my core that my room was handled and a confirming email came with my reservation and room number. WOW! That is the feeling I had when Caribbean Export was selecting seven designers for Caribbean Essence in London during the Olympics. In my mind I was on that list and I sure was.

My journey was indeed defining my purpose.

"Sonia Noel inspires me to be the best version of myself. I look up to you. I feel that more people should strive to have the strength and passion that you exemplify in everyday life. I have never been more proud to know someone and to call someone my role model."

Sohan Badal-
Designer/Dancer, Trinidad.

"I love Sonia's boldness, openness and the way she enjoys life."

Rawle Dundas - JMT
Speaker, Coach

65

Chapter 11

Conviction

We have to master our mindset of positive outcomes and prepare the mood instead of repairing, after the fact. Never forget the mind is a battle ground and we can defeat ourselves with our thoughts. This is conviction. Life is about being and doing and it's only through the doing you become. We all have those moments when we feel overwhelmed but when you know who you are you can snap back so fast. That can only happen if you have a better understanding of who you really are and not what people want you to be.

Even when things seem to be falling apart we need to maintain a positive mindset which is not always easy but that is how we get through those rough paths. The days we feel worse are the days we dress our best and pick ourselves up, with a reassuring message that God's delays are not God's denials. You wake up with a surplus energy when you truly have a vision for your life. Some days we need to use the reserve energy. Don't limit your beliefs of what you can do to disable you. We have to dare ourselves even if our wings are broken, we still can fly.

I decided I had enough of the Disney's fantastic view and needed to review some of the content from day one and some sleep in preparation for a magnificent day. The remaining days went by so fast with lots of WOW moments. The early morning church service was healing and gospel singer Martha Munizzi led the anointed worship session. Over 1000 came to the alter call. John said for him that is the most important part of the weekend because his teaching is bringing people to the kingdom.

Was it worth it? Hell, a resounding YES! This will go down as one the best birthday presents I ever had.

It was hard to contain myself when I got back home. I was overflowing with information and needed an outlet. I was telling everyone even my dogs that I missed them so much. How life changing it was and

I wished everyone could experience this new-found vitality. When you are on this journey you don't want to stop. A few weeks earlier, I saw on social media Lisa Nichols was having a four day conference in Atlanta and I had been thinking about it.

Before I think about another conference and leaving Guyana I needed to do a few things including calling Richard who is the creative director of Guyana Fashion Week (GFW). We were just a few months away from the week of activities and we needed to finalize plans. GFW is like my third child and probably cost me more money than my two daughters. lol. Many are surprised it lasted this long for it is the second longest fashion event in the Caribbean. I must confess many times I wanted to give up on that project. However, the main reason to continue, even under extremely difficult circumstances, is that we have to provide this platform for the young creative minds. The event has jumpstarted so many careers and that is enough reason.

Hosting my foster kids at the house before school reopens was another, because they always look forward to spending time with me and I didn't want to disappoint them. I was also looking forward to having dhal, fish, curry, callaloo and rice with my buddies Russell, Raquel, Merrano and Chris. Sometimes it is the little things that matter most. The number of kids varies but the most I ever had at once was 30 from two homes. They enjoyed having lunch while playing video games or watching movies.

That day I wanted our time to be different. Instead of them having lunch while in front of the TV I needed them at the table with me.

We said grace then I told them we would try something new today. "I am aware you all live in an orphanage but that is just a temporary position. You are bright, loving and have a place of greatness in the world. At this table we have CEOs, doctors, teachers, nurses and leaders in Government. Today I need us to eat with knives and forks instead of spoons because in the future you will be dining in high places. I believe in all of you that you can be anyone you want to be. You have a choice to try something new today or you have the option of a spoon." Can I tell you something? They all tried it and I was so proud of them.

Observing the pride and joy in their eyes reminded me of the same look I saw fifteen years ago from some kids in similar position. Mrs. Accra who managed the Joshua House Orphanage called me to share some precious photographs. The proceeds of my fashion shows went towards buying new mattresses, bed sheets and sleep wear. She said at nights, they were so excited for wearing something no one wore before them. The sheets were new and smelt so good and they were so elated. She couldn't resist taking pictures to share with me and I appreciated that more than she will ever know.

I knew what the cost was for, it was for the next event and I also was crazy to be thinking about another conference. I called my cousin Clemencio who is a big fan of Lisa and I told her I was going to the Speak & Write with Lisa in Atlanta and I will be in front, I am seeing myself in the front row.

She was screaming with excitement not knowing I had no idea how it was going to be a reality. There was an offer for two persons to register for less.

I called June Ann who lives in Atlanta but she could not make it. I needed to get creative so I sent the company a message if I can do a barter on outfits for Lisa for a free registration but that was not successful which just made me more determined. I needed to get the registration then I will figure the rest out. I know God provides for us by sending angels. I called a friend of mine who always commended me on my drive to do well with my life and with confidence, I stated "I need you to register me for Speak & Write in Atlanta". The link was sent and the registration was completed the same day. I was making some progress, all of which was fueled by my conviction.

I know some people may be thinking that she is a business woman and why can't she pay for this conference? Sometimes when you have a small business cash flow is not always what you want it to be.

I checked my Caribbean Airlines Frequent Flyer miles and I only had enough for a one-way ticket and you need a return ticket to go to countries you don't have permanent residence or some status. It made sense to stay at the hotel hosting the conference but the Marriott could be a bit pricey.

Living with Intention

"Dr. Sonia Noel has been an inspiration to me and since meeting her, my business has never been the same. She said to me, "you have not seen anything yet" and that was at the beginning of our first meeting. I am at the point of seeing things pertaining to business so differently."

> *- Lisa Gibson-CEO at Leisa Salon & Beauty Supplies, Guyana*

"Sonia lives a life full of creative energy! She lives fearlessly and passionately and embraces everyone she meets! She inspires me to live on purpose!"

> *- Jacque Faszekas -Life Coach Philadelphia*

Chapter 12

Liberation

Let me tell you how God works - the impossible becomes possible - and I feel a sense of liberation. I never visited the Speak and Write closed Facebook page but something led me there that day and the first message I saw was from Angie Lomax from California. Do you need a roommate? I wrote, I do. We started communicating and it was a relief to find out our view on life was in congruence and we finalized plans swiftly. I had my registration, a roommate and a one-way ticket to New York and Connections Travel provided the one to Atlanta. God was really providing angels because I called a friend and he agreed to assist with the room cost.

Selecting my wardrobe for my suitcase was a chore as I held the tiger flowing top in my hands and I thought that's what I would wear at the conference so here we come, front row at Speak & Write to make millions.

My daughter was worried I could not leave without a return ticket and she was reassured not to worry. As I was checking in, an agent was checking in the lady next to me and stated to her she could not enter the United States with a one-way ticket on a visitor's visa. The lady explained she had a return ticket with another airline and showed her the itinerary.

It may sound strange but I was not afraid knowing I only had a one-way ticket. My faith in God has added an unbelievable confidence to my demeanour. I called Marisca when I landed safe in the US. I needed to maximize this trip, so a colleague organized 'Conversations and Clothing' for me after the conference. I had VIP registration so I had the bonus day.

Angie, my roommate, was so funny and we hit it off instantly. It was exciting to meet other people in the lobby who were there for the conference. We were overjoyed for our first day to experience the possibilities. I did tell my cousin that I was going to be in front row and I even saw what I was wearing and it all was coming together. I was wearing a flowing animal top with lattice around the neckline and fitted chocolate pants with lattice edges at the bottom, from my collection. When I stepped off the elevators the compliments started and I felt extra special. They were asking about my signature braids which get attention everywhere. I have to thank my aunt, Corin Gibson for creating such a unique hairstyle for 15 years. The outfit from my collection was also receiving many compliments. They called me a goddess and I felt like one. The energy was explosive even before going in the room.

The attendees were mainly women and a few guys and we were interacting like old school friends.

VIP day started on a high note and we were dancing as the music was playing. The charismatic Matt Gil came on stage sharing his story of where he came from and so on. Lisa believed in him. He loves what he does and it shows. During the break, Matt and I connected and he told me he loves my energy and while he was on stage he was feeding off my energy.

We had a wonderful VIP lunch with the two power houses behind motivating the masses, Lisa Nichols and Susie Carter. The networking party that evening allowed us to know each other even better. I told Lisa that the stories that were most memorable from all the videos were the ones with her grandmother and the one with her son Jelani and the Tanker truck. She said that it is because I connected with her from the heart. She is truly a major inspiration, coming from being on public assistance to having a multimillion dollar business.

She reminds me a bit of Iyanla Vanzant, who I met at the Essence Festival. When Lisa told her story it was so touching and I was shocked to discover she attended the same conference forty-two times! WOW! That is commitment. She did not even have money to buy pampers for her son. She loves it when she says "does that resonate with you, say YES" and when it is deeper you say "YES! YES!", and the second yes has to be louder than the first. This double YES is our liberation.

One guy confessed that he had no place to stay so he slept in the lobby just to attend the conference and used the washroom to freshen up before coming in. Very impressive speakers were present, but Lisa is indeed the content queen. She captivates you. I love the personal and business relationship Lisa and Susie have cultivated.

"Sonia Noel has changed the way I view life. Over the years she made me desire to be a better woman and mom. She drives me to go deeper to find my greatness."

> *- Alana Edwards-Model,*
> *Barbados*

"The accomplishments of Sonia Noel can serve as an inspiration to everyone, especially young women, who live their daily lives with a passion to accomplish their dreams."

> *Mervyn Jordon*
>
> *–Businessman Arizona*

Chapter 13

Potential

You can really achieve your full potential in any field. You need a team that believes in you and your vision.

We can accomplish so much together if it does not matter who is credited and if we look at everyone as the MVP. The human resource is the most valuable resource we have. We cannot let money be the main motivation for the choices we make. When you love something and stick to it, the money follows.

"Good things happen to a team when a player takes the place where he adds the most value. Great things happen when all the players on the team take the role that maximizes their strengths—their talent, skill, and experience."

— John C. Maxwell,

I met Kathy Kidd, CEO of Kidd Marketing who assisted over 100 bestselling authors. I knew right away that I had to get out the book that was inside of me. I attended her breakout session and was sitting next to Hilda Bourne who is now like my sister. She was working on her book Nell's Nightmare. Hilda and I signed up with Kidd Marketing to make our books a reality.

Every day we had major breakthroughs and transformations with persons unmasking and unveiling and rediscovering ourselves. Many people felt relieved when discussing in the open, topics with which they felt uncomfortable, for a long time.

There is a feeling of liberation when you let it out and don't feel like people can judge you. This is the point when your potential can be maximized.

"I renew my spirit by releasing my guilt, fear and shame, acknowledging the truth and having accountability for my actions" - Lisa Nichols.

When we want something different we have to do something different.

Going through a personal development and leadership experience, especially when you were intentional is an awesome feeling. You go to sleep with a different energy and wake with a hunger you have never experienced before.

Les Brown is one of Lisa's mentors and mine. As one of the world's most renowned motivational speakers, Les Brown is a dynamic personality and highly-sought-after resource in business and professional circles for Fortune 500 CEOs, small business owners, non-profit and community leaders from all sectors of society looking to expand opportunity. For three decades he has not only studied the science of achievement, he's mastered it by interviewing hundreds of successful business leaders and collaborating with them in the boardroom translating theory into bottom-line results for his clients. One of his videos was played during the conference. I was saying how much I love Les and the lady two seats down told me she was going to his conference on the Monday.

That was great news because I thought he was in Atlanta. Then she said she was going to Cleveland, Ohio to his conference. My brain started working again. I have never been to Ohio and knew no one there but I felt the urge to be there. I got the conference info from Facebook and I called to inquire if any seats were available and there were seats. I did that in half an hour I registered without knowing how I was going to get there.

Looking at the prices for the tickets, I was wondering how can I grow wings to fly to Cleveland. lol. Apart from the high prices for the airline tickets there was no one who can get me there in time for the conference.

I called back the conference office and asked where else was Les speaking, and explained that because of my flight arrangements, I would not make it in time. They assured me that what I missed in the first session, I would regain it in the second conference.

So it was Ohio here I come. So I booked a one-way ticket to Ohio.

I left the conference early on the last day which was Sunday to attend the event Phoebe's Boutique was hosting for me that evening.

I departed early Monday morning heading to a place, I had never been before, but anxious for what greatness was possibly in store. The tiredness hit me as I fastened my seat belt. I had planned to change my outfit when I arrived at the airport but unfortunately my bags did not arrive. I went to the American Airline counter and gave them the address where the conference was being held. I came too far for anything to get in the way.

I hurried out and got a taxi and I was on my way feeling a little nervous about my bags because I was leaving Cleaveland, after the conference.

On my way I called Laura Lane, the person who told me about the event to tell her I was on my way. Would you believe she was not there, because she had become ill. A WOW moment for me. Then it hit me that she was just the messenger to get me to the conference, to use my potential strategically to get me to the conference. I got there, got my name tag and found a seat.

"You inspire me because you are a confident woman who is determined to turn failure into success. Miss Noel you are an extraordinary human who takes risks others would probably never consider taking. You make dreams a reality for people who can't see it becoming a possibility."

> *-Meleesa Payne –Bishop*
> *former Miss Guyana*
> *Universe/ MUA*
> *Choreographer, Guyana*

"Sonia has great compassion and seeks to understand before imparting wisdom. She provides counsel in a language all can understand."

- Christopher Bell

Real Estate Agent, Guyana

Chapter 14

Priceless

Les was saying you got to be HUNGRY, if you want to go after your greatness. He is electrifying. After listening to his tapes for so many years, here I was at his conference. I admired how down-to-earth he was and the special way he treated his mom. God, you certainly have plans for my life, I thought. He had a break just fifteen minutes after I arrived. I took the opportunity to introduce myself to him.

"Hi Mr. Brown, I am Sonia Noel from Guyana, South America." His response was funny. Where is that place, Sonia?

Do you know Brazil? I asked and he answered that he did know where Brazil was.

I explained that a border separated us. Then he said, "Let's take a selfie." lol.

We chatted for a few minutes then I went for some tea.

The program commenced after half an hour and the atmosphere was so electrifying my tiredness disappeared. At the end of the session I was happy I had made the decision to attend and I was even happier that I was one of the persons selected to have a late lunch with Les. We were able to ask him many questions and he answered them all. I love the answer when I asked him about his legacy and he said, "I Aspire to Inspire until I Expire!"

Sitting in such an intimate setting with Les Brown was priceless and it's a testimony that anything is possible.

Fortunately, my bags were there when we got back from lunch. The evening conference was great, as was anticipated. I was enjoying it so much that I forgot that I had not made plans to go to New York from there. The longer but cheaper way with the Greyhound bus was the logical choice. I made acquaintances everywhere I went so it was easy to hitch a ride to the bus stop.

That evening got better when Earnie, whom I met at the conference offered to take me to the Greyhound terminal. He suggested that I accompany him to a small event to chat with a group of women. Some of the best experiences are unplanned and that short stop was inspirational for all.

I did not feel as if it was my first time in Ohio and I was leaving on a high!

On the way to NY I realized I had a fever and was coughing. I know my body may be exhausted but couldn't get sick now, I was going to fight this. I drifted off after midnight as my thoughts went to the many amazing things which happened in a few months.

God's willing, I know one day I will be on stage opening for Les Brown and sharing the stage at John Maxwell LIVE2LEAD and Speak & Write.

I constantly think about Stephen Covey's beginning with the end in mind. There is a mental (first) creation, and a physical (second) creation. The physical creation follows the mental, just as a building follows a blueprint.

What do I desire for my eulogy to read?

My desire is to be remembered as a mighty woman of God who was shining her light in the darkness.

We are all in-transit and have a confirmed ticket to a destination, the time and date are what vary. How can we make the most of our time and make it count until the flights are announced? We have to give up who we are to become the persons we want to be. Those simple questions can change the way we think and do a lot of things.

"Do not go where the path may lead, go instead where there is no path and leave a trail."- Henry David Thoreau.

What trail are you leaving to make sure there is evidence that you existed? What will be different because you have passed through this earth?

When I think about the people who have inspired me like my grandmother, Winifred Gibson and mom, Claudia John, who found a way to always give from the little they had. They both took these words of the phenomenal Maya Angelou seriously, "when you learn, teach, when you get, give".

Larry Morrish, who was married to my dear friend Phillipa, was one of the richest men I had the privilege of meeting. When we mention words like rich and wealthy we think about material things but he had so much love to give to the world especially to the Bay Ridge community. He was the true meaning of a servant leader. With Larry, it was always about the people and never about him.

Auntie Lou, the oldest living person in my hometown Bartica, is now 95 and has touched hundreds of lives although she never had biological children. I always visit her when I go home and listen to her amazing stories about love and life.

I love, admire and respect a lot of people who are well known and some not well known. When I think about the people who are givers but are not famous, these names come to mind: Claudia John, Corin Gibson, dad- Alan John, Sandrina Timberman, Richard Young, Mr Nazar Mohamed, Apostle Claude Brooks, Pastor Carol Brooks Desiree De Florimonte, Leon Rutherford, Pastor Simon Harris, Denise Harris, Lorna Welchman-Neblette, Raquel Thomas Ceasar, Denise Dias, Michelle

Clarke, Alan Zaakir, Pat Lanford-Jordan, Sherif Barker, Gregory Cristiani, Lady Ira Lewis, Shiv Dindyal, Doris Rodney, Terrence Campbell, Edmon Braithwaite, Christine Neblette, Eion Willims, Joslyn Mendez, Hilda Bournes, Stan Harmon, Troy Cadogan Pastor Joseph Persaud, Phillipa Morrish, Pastor Ted and Shami Mahabir.

It gives me the urge to do more with great enthusiasm with examples like these in my life

I had promised Mr. Mohamed that I would pay him back and my word is my bond so when it was possible to make my first payment, I visited his office. He said, "That day when I paid the money it was a gift for you to continue to do well with your life. You have a good heart and you help people. I read your weekly column and you are making a difference in people's life. I am proud of you". I will NEVER forget this man. He has no idea the impact he has on my life. Experiences like these give me the urge to do more with great enthusiasm. Let's continue to create a relay method in adding value to lives. The effective handing over in any relay is the key for success. Your contribution may not be monetary but it may be mentorship. Whatever it is, you can contribute to the growth of humanity.

They are many verses in the bible that mentioned growth and even Jesus grew. One such is, "and Jesus grew in wisdom and stature, and in favour with God and man"- Luke 2:52. Someone once said you don't have to be great to start, but you have to start to be great.

I have found a way of feeling comfortable while being uncomfortable and being able to stand firm on my shaky legs and you can too.

I dare you to dig deeper and believe you are an original. I dare you to implement or accelerate that growth plan. I dare you to raise your standards.

We all should ask ourselves:

WHO AM I?

WHY AM I HERE?

FROM WHERE DID I COME?

WHAT CAN I DO?

WHERE AM I GOING?

Commit, Contribute, Celebrate

Join us for a FREE webinar on
LIVING WITH INTENTION
Interested persons email
livingwithintention11@gmail.com

"My dear Sonia, I am truly blessed and I feel very grateful for having you as a role model and a dear friend in my life. Seventeen years ago, when we first met I knew you were someone very special. The love and positivity you spread and the passion with which you do it, to make a difference in the world is so amazing. You are truly one of a kind and an incredibly gifted woman who inspires me to be the best version of myself. You put your heart and soul into helping others to surpass their goals. My dear Sonia keep on inspiring and I thank God for sending us his Angel to keep faith in mankind and to always believe in ourselves. Thank you for the life lessons, your patience, your strength and your love."

- Your lifetime friend,

Robin Corte, Holland

Commit, Contribute, Celebrate

By <u>Filisha</u> on November 29, 2017

Format: Kindle Edition   Verified Purchase

Wow! Words cannot describe how this book moved me, after reading I was in tears. To see such strength, determination, drive, focus and passion been demonstrated. As a young mother and entrepreneur many times when am faced with obstacles I feel like throwing in the towels, this book and what was shared by Dr. Noel ignited a fire within me. I felt empowered and more motivated than ever. I pressed the restart button that day.

By <u>Naomi Sodomin</u> on November 25, 2017

Format: Kindle Edition |Verified Purchase

WOW! This book is an amazing book in the sense it really shows you what can happen when you start living your life with intention. I highly recommend this book to anyone who's unclear about their future or they don't quite know what's next for them. Bravo Dr.Sonia Noel.

By <u>Kathy</u> on November 24, 2017

Format: Kindle Edition | Verified Purchase

I was waiting for this book to come out and I can't believe it.... It's finally here.... I know Dr. Noel personally and I admire her so much in fact I learned a lot from her... She also taught me to be strong and never let anyone say you can't do something. Always believe in yourself. I am so proud of her... I started reading and I can't put my kindle down.... Congrats Sonia!!!! Much love.... Muah!

By Omega C.on November 24, 2017

Format: Kindle Edition

WOW, what a source of renewed inspiration. So many great views on life from experiences that provides vision and determination. I recommend for all those in doubt of their future in life. Where there is a will there is always a way. Take one step at a time with faith but God being the leader. Bravo Dr.Sonia Noel.

By Dr. Monica Odwin-Sagala on November 25, 2017

Format: Kindle Edition

Captivating reading. I read from beginning to end at one go. A story of determination, perseverance, selflessness and faith while embracing and overcoming life's challenges. Truly inspiring and motivational. Congratulations Sonia.

By Amazon Customer Mayleen Burnett Wallaceon November 24, 2017

Format: Kindle Edition

|Verified Purchase

This book had me captivated from starting to ending. It shows with strength, vision and determination you can achieve the goals you set before you successfully. I compliment the author Ms Sonia Noel, hope a part two is in the making, all the very best, congratulations.

Living with Intention

Dr. SONIA E. NOEL D.H.L
Designer, Producer, Philanthropist, Life Coach

mobile: +592 684 8129
email: soniaenoel@gmail.com

office : +592 226 6554
web: www.sonianoel.com

Dr. Sonia Noel

is a passionate and industrious creative artist, with a fresh New World perspective on style. Sonia Noel is celebrating 20 years in the fashion industry. It took a combination of navigational skills and resilience to out-maneuver hurdles and literally row her own boat when the waters got rough. Small town girl from an interior community with a big dream who believed anything was possible, she charted a course that has taken her to the very top of her field. She celebrates her Amerindian roots, but she is no "woman of straw", yet she utilised this indigenous South American creativity and cosmopolitan Caribbean flair, to craft a unique fashion aesthetic that is identifiable, the Sonia Noel brand.

Her determined spirit pushes her to drive this creative industry forward, and she has become an exemplar and mentor to young creative minds, not only in Guyana, but throughout the region. She has been presented with many awards locally, regionally and internationally, for entrepreneurship, philanthropy, cultural ambassadorial services, advancing creative enterprise, promoting competitive-worthy fashion design and youth empowerment. Her designs can be worn from the each to the ballroom. Well-known names who have worn her designs are Maxi Priest, Miss Universe Leila Lopez, and Michelle Williams, formerly of Destiny's Child.

Originating from the village of Bartica, situated on a hamlet in the Essequibo River, far removed from the capital, where her dreams of becoming a fashion designer might have appeared far-fetched and illusory; she pioneered, persevered and eventually positioned her brand as a sought-after regional trendsetter, with international appeal. From her early collections, in Georgetown, relying on her geographic, architectural and Afro-Amerindian references, she has emerged as the quintessential Guyanese designer, influencing the Caribbean aesthetic, having shown her designs in the major capitals of the region and in the metropolises of the world, where there is an active Diaspora influence - London, Los Angeles, Atlanta, Washington, Boston, Texas, New Jersey, Miami New York, Toronto, Montreal and also in Spain, China and India. Sonia Noel is a true "*woman of substance*"!

Sonia Noel is the founder of Guyana Fashion Week, The Women's Association for Sustainable Development, The Women in Business Expo, Guyana Model Search, Designers' Portfolio and the Sonia Noel Foundation for Creative Arts.

Her work has been featured in numerous publications in the Caribbean and around the world. Richard Young.

Made in the USA
Columbia, SC
24 June 2018